SHADES OF BLUE

JOHN TESH & CONNIE SELLECCA

The fact that you are reading this book shows you already care.

Your donation will help provide the bare necessities of life for the people you will meet on these pages, the people in the Ampara district of Sri Lanka.

Thank you,

Connie, John, Gib, Prima

The island nation of Sri Lanka was one of the hardest hit by the Asian tsunami. As many as 37,000 people died there since an earthquake beneath the Indian Ocean set off mighty waves that swallowed coastlines across Asia. More than a half-million were injured in Sri Lanka, and five million people need help rebuilding their lives. Relief workers told us the shocking television images could not compare to the devastation they encountered.

We knew this from our radio interview with Bill Horan, the president and COO of Operation Blessing International, which was one of the first relief groups on location after the disaster hit Asia on December 26, 2004. Their relief teams have been providing emergency relief and critical medical aid

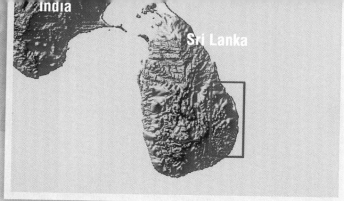

India

Sri Lanka

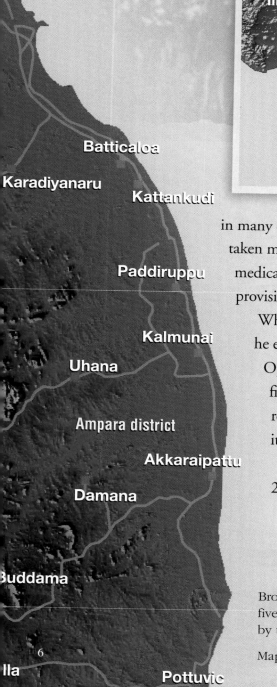

Batticaloa

Karadiyanaru

Kattankudi

Paddiruppu

Kalmunai

Uhana

Ampara district

Akkaraipattu

Damana

Buddama

Ila

Pottuvic

in many of the areas affected by the tsunami. They have taken millions of dollars worth of antibiotics and other medical supplies to Sri Lanka, where basic medical provisions were not available following the tsunami.

When we asked Horan what we could do to help, he extended an invitation for us to travel with Operation Blessing and see the relief efforts firsthand. We talked it over, and despite our very real concerns about what we might encounter, it felt right to go as a family.

So the four of us (John, Connie, along with 23-year-old son, Gib and 10-year-old daughter,

Brown color indicates areas between one and twenty-five meters in elevation affected or most likely affected by the tsunami.

Maps courtesy of UNOSAT satellite imagery.

Prima) spent the second week of January working with Operation Blessing in tsunami-ravaged Sri Lanka. The government has assigned Operation Blessing to meet the needs of survivors with food and medical supplies in nine refugee camps in Ampara, on the eastern coast of Sri Lanka. Kumar Periasamy, regional director of Operation Blessing in India, and his wife, Smita, have organized a medical team with doctors from Singapore to help these refugees as well as deliver food rations.

They are also working with an orphanage where the nuns, faced with a desperate situation, actually had to use the children's mattresses as emergency fuel in order to burn the bodies of the dead because of the fear of disease. Operation Blessing replaced the mattresses, adopted the orphanage, and continued to forge a bond with the nuns to form a valuable outpost and outreach for the orphans and the other children and families of Ampara.

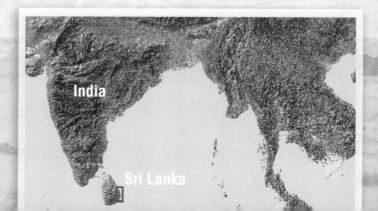

Once we arrived, we were taken directly to what remains of the fishing villages in Ampara, which are basically unlivable. When we visited the first camp, the children surrounded our van and pressed their faces up against the windows. It was surprising how much they smiled.

Fifty kids surrounded our van, and Gib twirled them around and did magic tricks for hours. We discovered that the boys in the relief camps desperately needed someone to play with them, and there was no one who could get them to play as hard as Gib. He was the "pied piper" and the little boys followed. It was the first time the adults had seen the kids smile and laugh, since the disaster.

Prima vanished in a sea of elementary school kids who demanded that she teach them English! The girls needed to be comforted and were eager to learn new dance steps. They were hungry for any kind of normalcy, and in Prima they found the perfect answer. She shattered the language barrier by speaking that special language only ten-year-olds understand.

Connie found herself helping the medical team and putting her arms around moms who had lost their kids. The mothers needed to cry, and in Connie they found a mother's heart to weep with them. And she couldn't go anywhere without three girls holding on each arm . . . flocks of kids . . . craving love.

The whole scene just melted our hearts, and for hours (at times

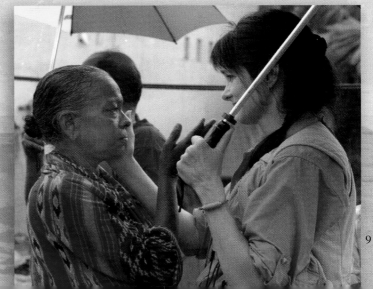

through an interpreter) we told the kids and the adults that the whole world was weeping for them. We assured them that the world would not forget, and that help was on the way to rebuild their homes and schools. We told them money is being raised. More medicine and supplies will arrive.

While we were in the camp helping distribute food and supplies with the folks from Operation Blessing, we kept hearing the same story over and over. As the local children grew more comfortable with us, the word

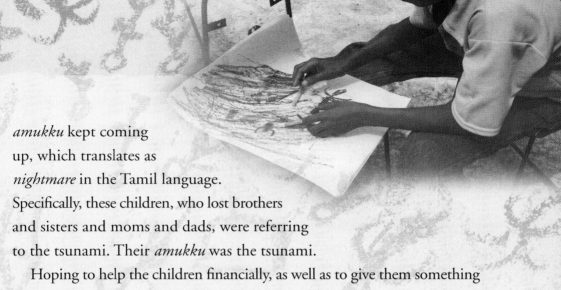

amukku kept coming
up, which translates as
nightmare in the Tamil language.
Specifically, these children, who lost brothers
and sisters and moms and dads, were referring
to the tsunami. Their *amukku* was the tsunami.

Hoping to help the children financially, as well as to give them something
fun to do, John came up with the idea of having the kids create artwork,
which we would bring back to the States and sell on their behalf. So Bill
Horan set out into town to buy paper and crayons.

However, Connie came up with the idea to take the artwork idea further
and ask all the kids in the camp to draw a picture of their *amukku*. Initially,
Bill and John were afraid that it might be too traumatic for the children,
and none of us were psychologists. But Connie said, "Trust me on this.

The kids need to get their feelings out, and they don't have an outlet."
So Bill and John deferred to a mother's instincts.

It took no time for the children to show us what was on their minds.
In the pictures they drew, you can see the horror on the faces of people
struggling to survive. You can see them trying to climb on top of houses.
Fishing boats are smashed to pieces, and children are running
for their lives. Of course, everything is
underwater—the trees, the houses, and the
people.

When we distributed the paper and
crayons, the kids scrambled and
fought for the blue crayons.
Everyone wanted to start with
shades of blue for the water. But,

as the children went about their task of creating these haunting pictures, they laughed and giggled, competing with one another to see who could come up with a masterpiece.

We all stood there with tears streaming down our cheeks, watching what only Connie knew would happen. The children of Sri Lanka were facing their deepest fears. We have all the stunning artwork, and on the pages that follow we're bringing it to you so you can get a peek into the hearts of these kids.

We've included our personal reflections from our time with these precious people whom we came to love.

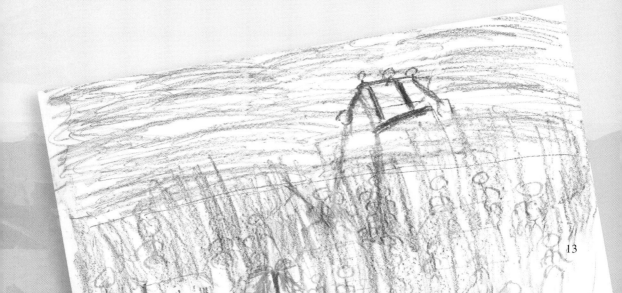

14

As we entered the villages,

we immediately recognized

the people's need to tell their stories.

I couldn't hold back the tears,

but there were none in their eyes.

Lost lives,
    lost dreams,
        lost hopes.

But still smiles.

Survival.

Reunited

A responsive smile . . . then the death-mask stare following me. I asked Kumar to translate.

The fisherman spoke softly and slowly,

"Everything . . .the sea took everything from me . . . my three children . . . my boat . . . my house."

He needed to tell his story.
I needed to tell him that we were here because we cared.

Not enough.

What could possibly be enough to rebuild the devastation?

"Are you afraid to stay?"

"Nothing to be afraid of now. The sea took it all. Nothing more for it to take."

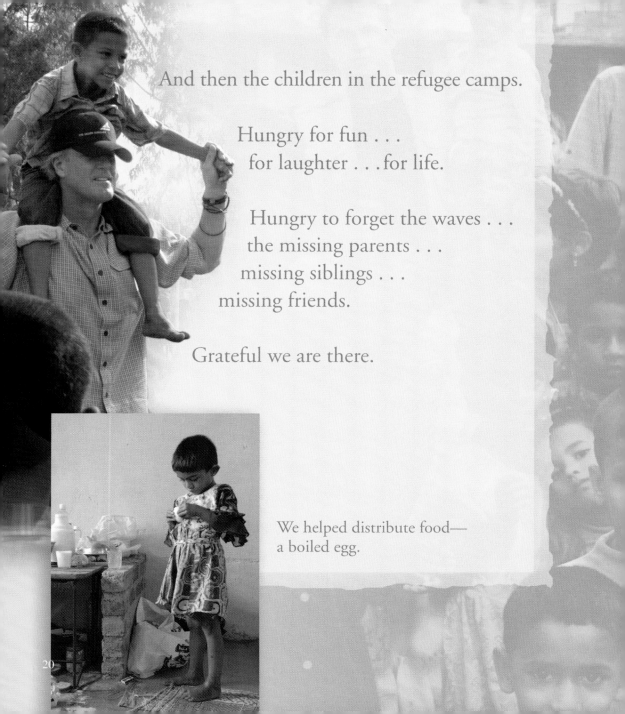

And then the children in the refugee camps.

Hungry for fun . . .
for laughter . . . for life.

Hungry to forget the waves . . .
the missing parents . . .
missing siblings . . .
missing friends.

Grateful we are there.

We helped distribute food—
a boiled egg.

20

I played with the kids today,
and we talked to some young adults.

They talked about their stories

and the family members they lost.

We had a translator.

I think this part of the trip was a great experience.

It made me be thankful for what I have.

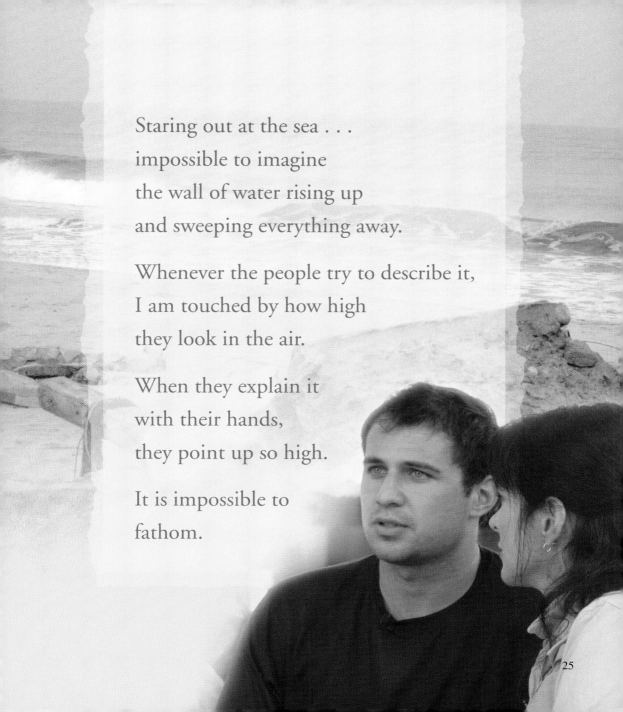

Staring out at the sea . . .
impossible to imagine
the wall of water rising up
and sweeping everything away.

Whenever the people try to describe it,
I am touched by how high
they look in the air.

When they explain it
with their hands,
they point up so high.

It is impossible to
fathom.

We walked amidst the rubble
on the beach in Akkaraipattu.

The debris was indescribable
bits and pieces of homes
bits and pieces of lives
strewn across the coast
ground into the sand.

Looking into the
people's eyes,
deep wells of pain,
and hearing their
stories firsthand
can only be understood by
experiencing it.

Two women who had been neighbors walk slowly, veils of sadness thickly lying on their faces.

It took fifteen days to find the courage to come back and see whatever might be left of their homes.

One was 'lucky' . . . to have found the body of her four-year-old daughter.

The other was not so 'lucky' . . .
still searching without hope to find her baby.

I watch as she finds a piece of clothing belonging to her child.

She clings to it . . .
I weep silently.

It's safer up high.

And there are the miracles.

There's 'The Coconut Baby.'

A three-month-old baby, Suha, hanging on a coconut tree for five hours, dangling by a piece of fabric from her mother's clothing.

Searching in despair for her infant, Sheila Shahudin looked up.

Miracles.

The converted elementary school is a surreal picture.

The fifth-grade classroom, a nursery for infants.
The kindergarten, a field hospital and treatment center.
And the second-grade classroom, a makeshift soup
kitchen.

And yet, the families have a supreme hope
that relief workers will bring cement and lumber
to build new homes and to help them somehow reclaim
their lives.

It is difficult to predict when that will happen.
I've seen the strength of these men and women . . .

the resilience of little boys and girls . . .
who should have lost hope long ago.

Look and see what I've seen in their eyes.
These faces will make it, and they know it.
They will make it through this.

A traumatized
teenaged girl
sits alone in a corner
seeing nothing, heeding nothing,
afraid of everything
in desperate need of help.

Thank God, it is coming.

It's a bittersweet feeling.

The aid has begun to arrive,
and the medical teams are working hard
to treat the sick and wounded.

But it is so heartbreaking to leave the kids,
still haunted by nightmares every night.

It's the wave . . . they are convinced the
tsunami will return.

Their lives will never be the same.

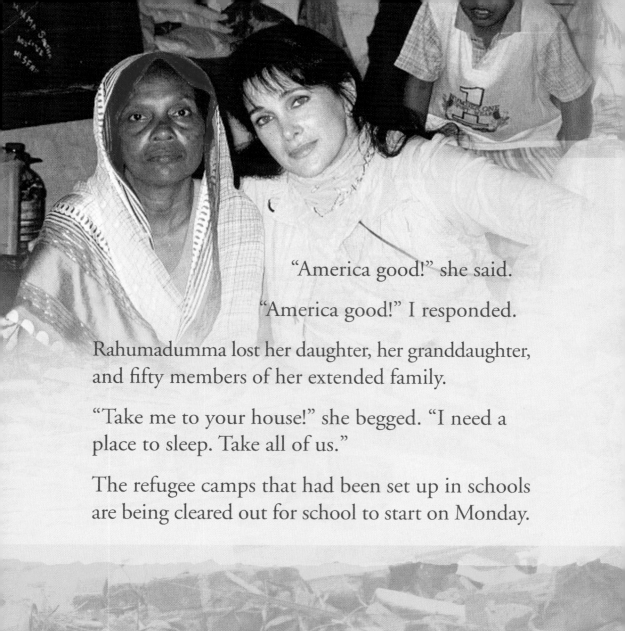

"America good!" she said.

"America good!" I responded.

Rahumadumma lost her daughter, her granddaughter, and fifty members of her extended family.

"Take me to your house!" she begged. "I need a place to sleep. Take all of us."

The refugee camps that had been set up in schools are being cleared out for school to start on Monday.

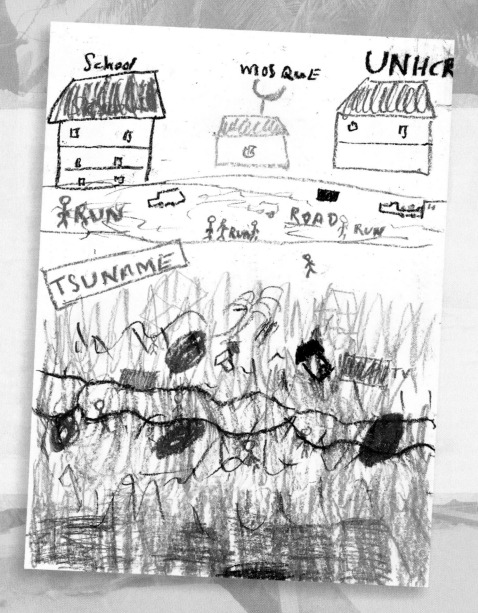

43

There is no place to go.

Millions are homeless.

Tens of thousands are injured.

Contaminated wells.
Shortage of food and shelter.
The bare necessities.
The difference between life and death
for the survivors.

"Don't forget us!"

That is one of the cries from the people.
They have a long road ahead of them.

"Don't forget us . . ."

Sea Urchins

My struggles seem petty now.
My complaints smaller
My life bigger.
Lonely maybe, but not alone.
Orphans in life, but not spirit

Then I drift like wood
Eight thousand plus miles
To mud and debris littered with shoelaces of
Tattered children not lucky enough to be woken

Drenched nightmares of
Giant chasing walls.
They float in my dreams
Haunting drifting angels
Fingertips just out of my reach.

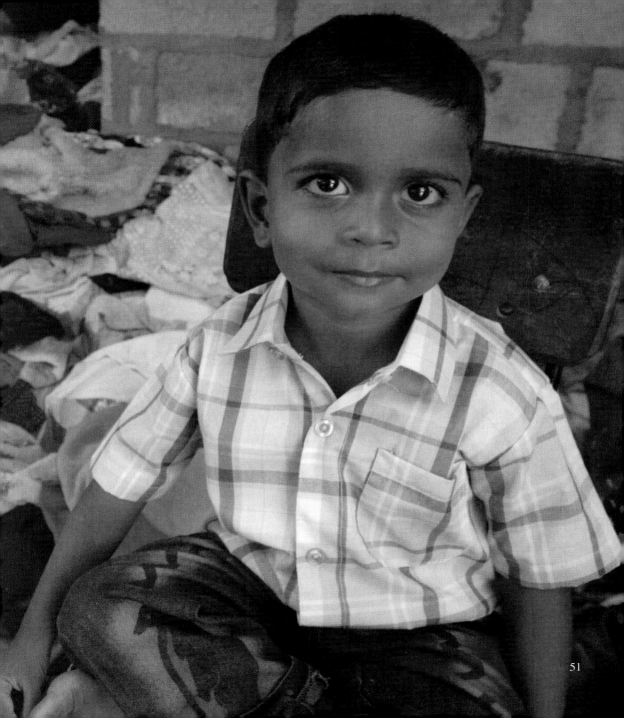

It isn't good enough just to have faith. Faith that doesn't show itself by good deeds is no faith at all—it is dead and useless.*

There is no limit to the amount of attention needed here.

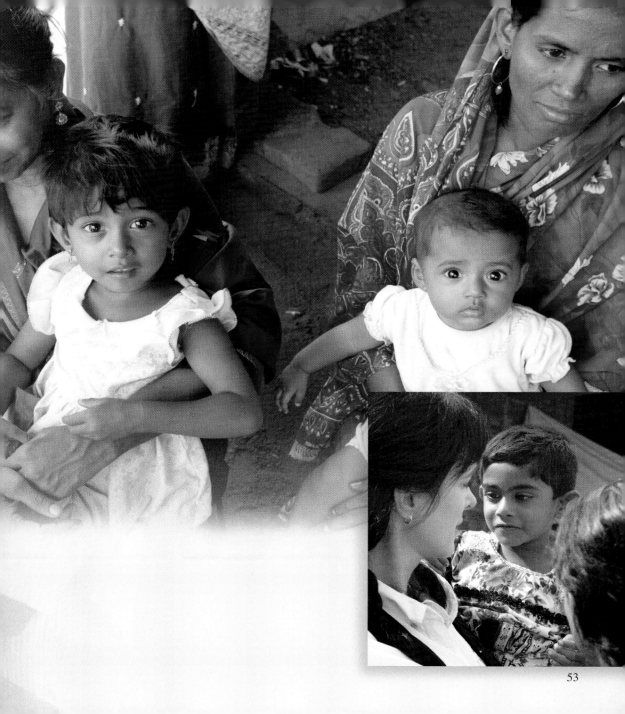

He will wipe every tear from their eyes.

There will be no more death or

mourning or crying or pain, for the old

order of things has passed away.*

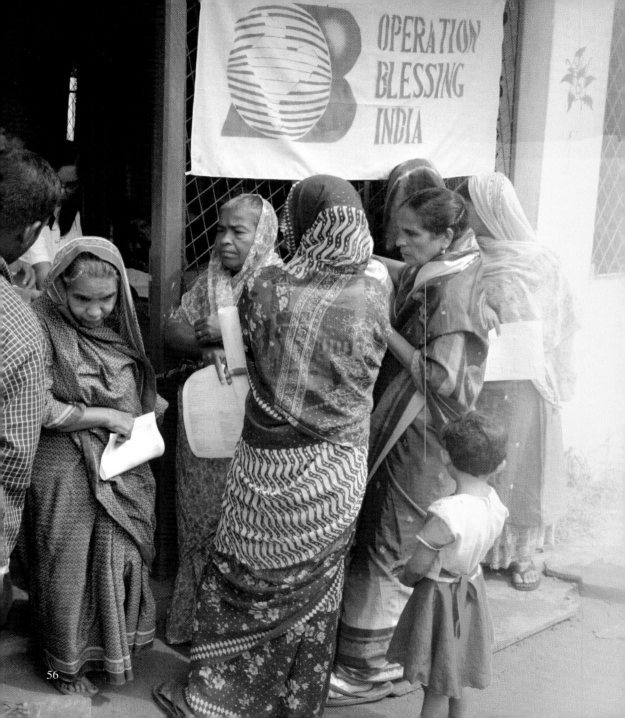

Operation Blessing International Relief and Development Corporation (OBI) is a non-profit 501 (c) (3) humanitarian organization based in Virginia Beach, Virginia. Since 1978, OBI has touched the lives of more than 175 million people in 96 countries and all 50 states, providing goods and services valued at more than $750 million.

OBI is a member of the Association of Evangelical Relief and Development Organizations (AERDO) and is registered with the Federal Emergency Management Association (FEMA), the United States Agency for International Development (USAID), and the Evangelical Council for Financial Accountability (ECFA).

Write to us at: Teshmedia
PO Box 6010-721
Sherman Oaks, CA 91413

1-877-801-4995
www.Tesh.com

Art Therapy Notes

Vanessa Womack, M.A.

Master of Arts Degree in Psychology/Art Therapy

Cover: This child most likely witnessed a great deal of death. Notice the people struggling in the water. This child seems to notice and remember a wide array of details from the tragic events.

Page 16: This drawing's focus is centered on what seem to be two large dead people with missing limbs, symbolizing, perhaps, both personal and widespread death to this particular child. However, what stands out unique in this depiction is the bright, safe, lively people surrounding the dead. These warm outskirts of the artwork are brave symbols of strength and hope protecting this child's deep-felt wounds.

Page 18: Boats floating on top of the water show optimism and a focus on what's living. The emphasis on the living—people in trees and on houses—leads one to believe that the artist is focusing on survival. The one body that looks dead could be someone significant to the artist or a representation of death.

Page 21: In one word: Hope. The colors feel hopeful, and the survivors are colorful, signaling optimism. The living outnumber the images of death. Given the size of the representation of the one large dead person, this could be someone close to the artist or a representation of all who lost their lives.

Page 27: A detail of note in this drawing is the circles surrounding the people underwater. Some heads are above the circle and some are below, but this child seems to view the water as something binding. Also note the broken tree that is still green. This tree may symbolize the hope for regrowth after the tragedy.

Page 32: This drawing does not emphasize survival and, therefore, may seem less hopeful than the others to the onlooker. Everyone and everything are underwater. The artist is drawing from a distance and seems detached from the event.

Page 38: The colors in this drawing present some interesting questions. The purple color of the house and the boat rescuing the survivors makes these items stand out. Some questions to consider when looking at the drawing: Do they have special meaning to the artist? Why is there purple shading in the water that appears safe? Could it also be a sign of hope and survival? Is it the part of the water where the child was rescued? The trees are green, even while underwater. Does it mean that the artist is focusing on the tree still being alive?

Page 52: The large, central, colorful figure may be the child who drew the picture. The trees are still green, the color of growth, and therefore hopeful. Boats are floating in the background, and the artist represents more than destruction in the events that transpired.

We'd like to thank the following "Underwriters" for their generous support and contributions:

TITLE

PLATINUM

Ken & Katrina Carlson

Mac & Susan Dunwoody

 INORecords

Joleen Julis

Mitchell Julis

Hewlett, Sheree, Samantha & Ashley Kent

Thomas Lane

Joe White & Kanakuk Kamps

GOLD

In honor of Jordon Elizabeth
   & Joshua Christian Bensen

Dial Global

The Westland School

SILVER

Randy Campbell &
   Loralee Campbell

Bob & Barbara Mancini
   & Family

St. Paul Elder Services in
   Kaukauna, Wisconsin

Linde & Kessa Thurman

To order more books or to find out how you can get your business, school, or club involved in this project please, visit Tesh.com

Pure and lasting religion in the sight of God our Father means that we must care for orphans and widows in their troubles...*